50 Italian Ice Cream Recipes for Home

By: Kelly Johnson

Table of Contents

- Vanilla Gelato
- Chocolate Gelato
- Stracciatella Gelato
- Pistachio Gelato
- Hazelnut Gelato
- Tiramisu Gelato
- Coffee Gelato
- Amaretto Gelato
- Lemon Sorbet
- Raspberry Sorbet
- Mango Sorbet
- Strawberry Sorbet
- Blood Orange Sorbet
- Limoncello Sorbet
- Chocolate Hazelnut Gelato
- Bacio Gelato (Chocolate and Hazelnut)
- Fior di Latte Gelato
- Cioccolato Gelato
- Cappuccino Gelato
- Salted Caramel Gelato
- Coconut Gelato
- Almond Gelato
- Cherry Gelato
- Watermelon Sorbet
- Pineapple Sorbet
- Kiwi Sorbet
- Passion Fruit Sorbet
- Melon Sorbet
- White Peach Sorbet
- Pear Sorbet
- Fig Gelato
- Walnut Gelato
- Biscotti Gelato
- Marsala Gelato
- Panna Cotta Gelato

- Ricotta Gelato
- Yogurt Gelato
- Basil Gelato
- Lavender Gelato
- Rose Gelato
- Saffron Gelato
- Mint Gelato
- Cardamom Gelato
- Pistachio Rosewater Gelato
- Cherry Amaretto Gelato
- Orange Campari Gelato
- Honey Ricotta Gelato
- Espresso Granita
- Amarena Gelato (Sour Cherry)
- Zabaione Gelato

Vanilla Gelato

Ingredients:

- 2 cups whole milk
- 1 cup heavy cream
- 3/4 cup granulated sugar
- 1 vanilla bean (or 2 teaspoons vanilla extract)
- 6 large egg yolks

Instructions:

1. In a medium saucepan, combine the milk, heavy cream, and half of the sugar. If using a vanilla bean, split it lengthwise with a knife and scrape out the seeds. Add both the seeds and the bean pod to the saucepan. Heat the mixture over medium heat, stirring occasionally, until it reaches a simmer. Remove from heat and let it steep for 15-20 minutes to infuse the flavors.
2. In a separate bowl, whisk the egg yolks with the remaining sugar until pale and slightly thickened.
3. Remove the vanilla bean pod from the milk mixture and discard (if using vanilla extract, add it now). Slowly pour about 1/2 cup of the warm milk mixture into the egg yolks, whisking constantly to temper the eggs.
4. Gradually pour the tempered egg mixture back into the saucepan with the remaining milk mixture, whisking constantly.
5. Cook the mixture over medium-low heat, stirring constantly with a wooden spoon or spatula, until it thickens slightly and coats the back of the spoon (about 170-175°F or 77-80°C on an instant-read thermometer). Do not let it boil.
6. Strain the mixture through a fine-mesh sieve into a clean bowl to remove any bits of cooked egg or vanilla bean residue.
7. Cover the bowl with plastic wrap, pressing it directly onto the surface of the custard to prevent a skin from forming. Refrigerate until completely chilled, preferably overnight.
8. Once chilled, churn the custard in an ice cream maker according to the manufacturer's instructions until it reaches a soft-serve consistency.
9. Transfer the gelato to an airtight container and freeze for at least 2 hours or until firm before serving.

Enjoy your homemade vanilla gelato!

Chocolate Gelato

Ingredients:

- 2 cups whole milk
- 1 cup heavy cream
- 3/4 cup granulated sugar
- 1/2 cup unsweetened cocoa powder
- 4 ounces dark chocolate (about 70% cocoa), finely chopped
- 4 large egg yolks
- 1 teaspoon vanilla extract
- Pinch of salt

Instructions:

1. In a medium saucepan, combine the milk, heavy cream, sugar, and cocoa powder. Heat over medium heat, stirring occasionally, until the mixture starts to simmer and the cocoa powder and sugar are fully dissolved.
2. Remove the saucepan from heat and add the chopped dark chocolate. Stir until the chocolate is completely melted and the mixture is smooth. Set aside.
3. In a separate bowl, whisk the egg yolks until smooth.
4. Slowly pour about 1/2 cup of the warm chocolate mixture into the egg yolks, whisking constantly to temper the eggs.
5. Gradually pour the tempered egg mixture back into the saucepan with the remaining chocolate mixture, whisking constantly.
6. Cook the mixture over medium-low heat, stirring constantly with a wooden spoon or spatula, until it thickens slightly and coats the back of the spoon (about 170-175°F or 77-80°C on an instant-read thermometer). Do not let it boil.
7. Remove from heat and stir in the vanilla extract and a pinch of salt.
8. Strain the mixture through a fine-mesh sieve into a clean bowl to remove any bits of cooked egg.
9. Cover the bowl with plastic wrap, pressing it directly onto the surface of the custard to prevent a skin from forming. Refrigerate until completely chilled, preferably overnight.
10. Once chilled, churn the custard in an ice cream maker according to the manufacturer's instructions until it reaches a soft-serve consistency.
11. Transfer the gelato to an airtight container and freeze for at least 2 hours or until firm before serving.

Enjoy your homemade chocolate gelato, rich and creamy with deep chocolate flavor!

Stracciatella Gelato

Ingredients:

- 2 cups whole milk
- 1 cup heavy cream
- 3/4 cup granulated sugar
- 4 ounces dark chocolate (about 70% cocoa), finely chopped
- 4 large egg yolks
- 1 teaspoon vanilla extract

Instructions:

1. In a medium saucepan, combine the milk, heavy cream, and half of the sugar. Heat over medium heat, stirring occasionally, until the mixture starts to simmer and the sugar is fully dissolved.
2. Remove the saucepan from heat and add the chopped dark chocolate. Stir until the chocolate is completely melted and the mixture is smooth. Set aside.
3. In a separate bowl, whisk the egg yolks with the remaining sugar until pale and slightly thickened.
4. Slowly pour about 1/2 cup of the warm chocolate mixture into the egg yolks, whisking constantly to temper the eggs.
5. Gradually pour the tempered egg mixture back into the saucepan with the remaining chocolate mixture, whisking constantly.
6. Cook the mixture over medium-low heat, stirring constantly with a wooden spoon or spatula, until it thickens slightly and coats the back of the spoon (about 170-175°F or 77-80°C on an instant-read thermometer). Do not let it boil.
7. Remove from heat and stir in the vanilla extract.
8. Let the mixture cool to room temperature, then cover the bowl with plastic wrap, pressing it directly onto the surface of the custard to prevent a skin from forming. Refrigerate until completely chilled, preferably overnight.
9. Once chilled, churn the custard in an ice cream maker according to the manufacturer's instructions until it reaches a soft-serve consistency.
10. During the last few minutes of churning, drizzle in melted dark chocolate in thin ribbons. The churning action will break the chocolate into small pieces, creating the signature stracciatella effect.
11. Transfer the gelato to an airtight container and freeze for at least 2 hours or until firm before serving.

Enjoy your homemade stracciatella gelato, with its creamy base and delightful chocolate shards throughout!

Pistachio Gelato

Ingredients:

- 2 cups whole milk
- 1 cup heavy cream
- 3/4 cup granulated sugar
- 1 cup shelled pistachios, unsalted
- 4 large egg yolks
- 1 teaspoon almond extract
- Pinch of salt

Instructions:

1. In a blender or food processor, grind the pistachios until finely chopped but not turned into a paste. Set aside.
2. In a medium saucepan, combine the milk, heavy cream, and half of the sugar. Heat over medium heat, stirring occasionally, until the mixture starts to simmer and the sugar is fully dissolved.
3. Remove the saucepan from heat and stir in the ground pistachios. Let the mixture steep for about 20-30 minutes to infuse the pistachio flavor.
4. After steeping, strain the mixture through a fine-mesh sieve into a clean bowl, pressing on the solids to extract as much flavor as possible. Discard the solids.
5. In a separate bowl, whisk the egg yolks with the remaining sugar until pale and slightly thickened.
6. Slowly pour about 1/2 cup of the warm pistachio-infused milk mixture into the egg yolks, whisking constantly to temper the eggs.
7. Gradually pour the tempered egg mixture back into the saucepan with the remaining pistachio-infused milk mixture, whisking constantly.
8. Cook the mixture over medium-low heat, stirring constantly with a wooden spoon or spatula, until it thickens slightly and coats the back of the spoon (about 170-175°F or 77-80°C on an instant-read thermometer). Do not let it boil.
9. Remove from heat and stir in the almond extract and a pinch of salt.
10. Let the mixture cool to room temperature, then cover the bowl with plastic wrap, pressing it directly onto the surface of the custard to prevent a skin from forming. Refrigerate until completely chilled, preferably overnight.
11. Once chilled, churn the custard in an ice cream maker according to the manufacturer's instructions until it reaches a soft-serve consistency.
12. Transfer the gelato to an airtight container and freeze for at least 2 hours or until firm before serving.

Enjoy your homemade pistachio gelato, with its creamy texture and delicious nutty flavor!

Hazelnut Gelato

Ingredients:

- 2 cups whole milk
- 1 cup heavy cream
- 3/4 cup granulated sugar
- 1 cup hazelnuts, toasted and skins removed
- 4 large egg yolks
- 1 teaspoon vanilla extract
- Pinch of salt

Instructions:

1. In a blender or food processor, grind the toasted hazelnuts until finely chopped. Set aside.
2. In a medium saucepan, combine the milk, heavy cream, and half of the sugar. Heat over medium heat, stirring occasionally, until the mixture starts to simmer and the sugar is fully dissolved.
3. Remove the saucepan from heat and stir in the ground hazelnuts. Let the mixture steep for about 20-30 minutes to infuse the hazelnut flavor.
4. After steeping, strain the mixture through a fine-mesh sieve into a clean bowl, pressing on the solids to extract as much flavor as possible. Discard the solids.
5. In a separate bowl, whisk the egg yolks with the remaining sugar until pale and slightly thickened.
6. Slowly pour about 1/2 cup of the warm hazelnut-infused milk mixture into the egg yolks, whisking constantly to temper the eggs.
7. Gradually pour the tempered egg mixture back into the saucepan with the remaining hazelnut-infused milk mixture, whisking constantly.
8. Cook the mixture over medium-low heat, stirring constantly with a wooden spoon or spatula, until it thickens slightly and coats the back of the spoon (about 170-175°F or 77-80°C on an instant-read thermometer). Do not let it boil.
9. Remove from heat and stir in the vanilla extract and a pinch of salt.
10. Let the mixture cool to room temperature, then cover the bowl with plastic wrap, pressing it directly onto the surface of the custard to prevent a skin from forming. Refrigerate until completely chilled, preferably overnight.
11. Once chilled, churn the custard in an ice cream maker according to the manufacturer's instructions until it reaches a soft-serve consistency.
12. Transfer the gelato to an airtight container and freeze for at least 2 hours or until firm before serving.

Enjoy your homemade hazelnut gelato, with its creamy texture and rich hazelnut flavor!

Tiramisu Gelato

Ingredients:

- 2 cups whole milk
- 1 cup heavy cream
- 3/4 cup granulated sugar
- 4 large egg yolks
- 1/4 cup mascarpone cheese
- 1/4 cup brewed espresso or strong coffee, cooled
- 2 tablespoons coffee liqueur (such as Kahlua), optional
- 1 teaspoon vanilla extract
- 1/2 cup ladyfinger cookies, crushed

Instructions:

1. In a medium saucepan, combine the milk, heavy cream, and half of the sugar. Heat over medium heat, stirring occasionally, until the mixture starts to simmer and the sugar is fully dissolved.
2. In a separate bowl, whisk the egg yolks with the remaining sugar until pale and slightly thickened.
3. Slowly pour about 1/2 cup of the warm milk mixture into the egg yolks, whisking constantly to temper the eggs.
4. Gradually pour the tempered egg mixture back into the saucepan with the remaining milk mixture, whisking constantly.
5. Cook the mixture over medium-low heat, stirring constantly with a wooden spoon or spatula, until it thickens slightly and coats the back of the spoon (about 170-175°F or 77-80°C on an instant-read thermometer). Do not let it boil.
6. Remove from heat and whisk in the mascarpone cheese until smooth.
7. Stir in the brewed espresso or coffee, coffee liqueur (if using), and vanilla extract. Mix until well combined.
8. Let the mixture cool to room temperature, then cover the bowl with plastic wrap, pressing it directly onto the surface of the custard to prevent a skin from forming. Refrigerate until completely chilled, preferably overnight.
9. Once chilled, churn the custard in an ice cream maker according to the manufacturer's instructions until it reaches a soft-serve consistency.
10. During the last few minutes of churning, add the crushed ladyfinger cookies and let them mix into the gelato.
11. Transfer the tiramisu gelato to an airtight container and freeze for at least 2 hours or until firm before serving.

Enjoy your homemade tiramisu gelato, with its rich coffee flavor and hints of mascarpone and ladyfingers!

Coffee Gelato

Ingredients:

- 2 cups whole milk
- 1 cup heavy cream
- 3/4 cup granulated sugar
- 1/4 cup brewed espresso or strong coffee, cooled
- 4 large egg yolks
- 1 teaspoon vanilla extract

Instructions:

1. In a medium saucepan, combine the milk, heavy cream, and half of the sugar. Heat over medium heat, stirring occasionally, until the mixture starts to simmer and the sugar is fully dissolved.
2. In a separate bowl, whisk the egg yolks with the remaining sugar until pale and slightly thickened.
3. Slowly pour about 1/2 cup of the warm milk mixture into the egg yolks, whisking constantly to temper the eggs.
4. Gradually pour the tempered egg mixture back into the saucepan with the remaining milk mixture, whisking constantly.
5. Cook the mixture over medium-low heat, stirring constantly with a wooden spoon or spatula, until it thickens slightly and coats the back of the spoon (about 170-175°F or 77-80°C on an instant-read thermometer). Do not let it boil.
6. Remove from heat and stir in the brewed espresso or coffee and vanilla extract. Mix until well combined.
7. Let the mixture cool to room temperature, then cover the bowl with plastic wrap, pressing it directly onto the surface of the custard to prevent a skin from forming. Refrigerate until completely chilled, preferably overnight.
8. Once chilled, churn the custard in an ice cream maker according to the manufacturer's instructions until it reaches a soft-serve consistency.
9. Transfer the coffee gelato to an airtight container and freeze for at least 2 hours or until firm before serving.

Enjoy your homemade coffee gelato, with its smooth texture and bold coffee flavor!

Amaretto Gelato

Ingredients:

- 2 cups whole milk
- 1 cup heavy cream
- 3/4 cup granulated sugar
- 4 large egg yolks
- 1/4 cup amaretto liqueur
- 1 teaspoon almond extract

Instructions:

1. In a medium saucepan, combine the milk, heavy cream, and half of the sugar. Heat over medium heat, stirring occasionally, until the mixture starts to simmer and the sugar is fully dissolved.
2. In a separate bowl, whisk the egg yolks with the remaining sugar until pale and slightly thickened.
3. Slowly pour about 1/2 cup of the warm milk mixture into the egg yolks, whisking constantly to temper the eggs.
4. Gradually pour the tempered egg mixture back into the saucepan with the remaining milk mixture, whisking constantly.
5. Cook the mixture over medium-low heat, stirring constantly with a wooden spoon or spatula, until it thickens slightly and coats the back of the spoon (about 170-175°F or 77-80°C on an instant-read thermometer). Do not let it boil.
6. Remove from heat and stir in the amaretto liqueur and almond extract. Mix until well combined.
7. Let the mixture cool to room temperature, then cover the bowl with plastic wrap, pressing it directly onto the surface of the custard to prevent a skin from forming. Refrigerate until completely chilled, preferably overnight.
8. Once chilled, churn the custard in an ice cream maker according to the manufacturer's instructions until it reaches a soft-serve consistency.
9. Transfer the amaretto gelato to an airtight container and freeze for at least 2 hours or until firm before serving.

Enjoy your homemade amaretto gelato, with its creamy texture and delightful almond flavor enhanced by the liqueur!

Lemon Sorbet

Ingredients:

- 2 cups water
- 1 cup granulated sugar
- 1 cup freshly squeezed lemon juice (about 4-5 lemons)
- Zest of 1 lemon

Instructions:

1. In a small saucepan, combine the water and sugar. Heat over medium heat, stirring occasionally, until the sugar is completely dissolved. This creates a simple syrup. Remove from heat and let it cool to room temperature.
2. Once the syrup is cooled, stir in the freshly squeezed lemon juice and lemon zest. Mix well.
3. Pour the mixture into an ice cream maker and churn according to the manufacturer's instructions until it reaches a slushy, sorbet-like consistency. This usually takes about 20-25 minutes.
4. Transfer the lemon sorbet to an airtight container and freeze for at least 2 hours to firm up before serving.
5. Serve the lemon sorbet in chilled bowls or cones, garnished with a twist of lemon zest or fresh mint leaves if desired.

Enjoy your homemade lemon sorbet, with its bright citrus flavor and refreshing texture!

Raspberry Sorbet

Ingredients:

- 4 cups fresh or frozen raspberries
- 1 cup water
- 1 cup granulated sugar
- 2 tablespoons freshly squeezed lemon juice

Instructions:

1. In a small saucepan, combine the water and sugar. Heat over medium heat, stirring occasionally, until the sugar is completely dissolved. This creates a simple syrup. Remove from heat and let it cool to room temperature.
2. In a blender or food processor, blend the raspberries until smooth.
3. Strain the raspberry puree through a fine-mesh sieve into a bowl to remove the seeds. You should have about 2 cups of raspberry puree.
4. Stir the cooled simple syrup and freshly squeezed lemon juice into the raspberry puree until well combined.
5. Pour the mixture into an ice cream maker and churn according to the manufacturer's instructions until it reaches a slushy, sorbet-like consistency. This usually takes about 20-25 minutes.
6. Transfer the raspberry sorbet to an airtight container and freeze for at least 2 hours to firm up before serving.
7. Serve the raspberry sorbet in chilled bowls or cones, garnished with fresh raspberries or mint leaves if desired.

Enjoy your homemade raspberry sorbet, with its vibrant color and delicious berry flavor!

Mango Sorbet

Ingredients:

- 4 cups ripe mango, peeled and diced (about 4-5 medium mangoes)
- 1 cup water
- 3/4 cup granulated sugar
- 2 tablespoons freshly squeezed lime or lemon juice

Instructions:

1. In a small saucepan, combine the water and sugar. Heat over medium heat, stirring occasionally, until the sugar is completely dissolved. This creates a simple syrup. Remove from heat and let it cool to room temperature.
2. In a blender or food processor, puree the diced mango until smooth.
3. Strain the mango puree through a fine-mesh sieve into a bowl to remove any fibrous bits or strings. You should have about 3 cups of mango puree.
4. Stir the cooled simple syrup and freshly squeezed lime or lemon juice into the mango puree until well combined.
5. Pour the mixture into an ice cream maker and churn according to the manufacturer's instructions until it reaches a slushy, sorbet-like consistency. This usually takes about 20-25 minutes.
6. Transfer the mango sorbet to an airtight container and freeze for at least 2 hours to firm up before serving.
7. Serve the mango sorbet in chilled bowls or cones, garnished with a slice of fresh mango or a sprig of mint if desired.

Enjoy your homemade mango sorbet, with its tropical taste and smooth texture!

Strawberry Sorbet

Ingredients:

- 4 cups fresh strawberries, hulled and halved
- 1 cup water
- 3/4 cup granulated sugar
- 2 tablespoons freshly squeezed lemon juice

Instructions:

1. In a small saucepan, combine the water and sugar. Heat over medium heat, stirring occasionally, until the sugar is completely dissolved. This creates a simple syrup. Remove from heat and let it cool to room temperature.
2. In a blender or food processor, puree the strawberries until smooth.
3. Strain the strawberry puree through a fine-mesh sieve into a bowl to remove the seeds. You should have about 3 cups of strawberry puree.
4. Stir the cooled simple syrup and freshly squeezed lemon juice into the strawberry puree until well combined.
5. Pour the mixture into an ice cream maker and churn according to the manufacturer's instructions until it reaches a slushy, sorbet-like consistency. This usually takes about 20-25 minutes.
6. Transfer the strawberry sorbet to an airtight container and freeze for at least 2 hours to firm up before serving.
7. Serve the strawberry sorbet in chilled bowls or cones, garnished with fresh strawberries or mint leaves if desired.

Enjoy your homemade strawberry sorbet, with its vibrant color and delicious berry flavor!

Blood Orange Sorbet

Ingredients:

- 4 cups fresh blood orange juice (from about 8-10 blood oranges)
- 1 cup water
- 3/4 cup granulated sugar
- Zest of 1 blood orange (optional, for extra flavor)
- 2 tablespoons freshly squeezed lemon juice

Instructions:

1. In a small saucepan, combine the water and sugar. Heat over medium heat, stirring occasionally, until the sugar is completely dissolved. This creates a simple syrup. Remove from heat and let it cool to room temperature.
2. While the syrup is cooling, juice the blood oranges until you have about 4 cups of juice. Strain the juice through a fine-mesh sieve to remove any pulp or seeds. If using zest, grate the zest from one blood orange and set aside.
3. In a large bowl, combine the blood orange juice, cooled simple syrup, freshly squeezed lemon juice, and optional blood orange zest. Stir well to combine.
4. Pour the mixture into an ice cream maker and churn according to the manufacturer's instructions until it reaches a slushy, sorbet-like consistency. This typically takes about 20-25 minutes.
5. Transfer the blood orange sorbet to an airtight container and freeze for at least 2 hours to firm up before serving.
6. Serve the blood orange sorbet in chilled bowls or cones, garnished with a twist of blood orange zest or a slice of blood orange if desired.

Enjoy your homemade blood orange sorbet, with its bright citrus flavor and beautiful color!

Limoncello Sorbet

Ingredients:

- 2 cups water
- 1 cup granulated sugar
- 1 cup freshly squeezed lemon juice (about 4-5 lemons)
- Zest of 2 lemons
- 1/2 cup limoncello liqueur

Instructions:

1. In a small saucepan, combine the water and sugar. Heat over medium heat, stirring occasionally, until the sugar is completely dissolved. This creates a simple syrup. Remove from heat and let it cool to room temperature.
2. While the syrup is cooling, zest the lemons using a fine grater or zester, being careful to avoid the bitter white pith.
3. In a large bowl, combine the cooled simple syrup, freshly squeezed lemon juice, lemon zest, and limoncello liqueur. Stir well to combine.
4. Pour the mixture into an ice cream maker and churn according to the manufacturer's instructions until it reaches a slushy, sorbet-like consistency. This usually takes about 20-25 minutes.
5. Transfer the limoncello sorbet to an airtight container and freeze for at least 2 hours to firm up before serving.
6. Serve the limoncello sorbet in chilled bowls or cones, garnished with a twist of lemon zest or a slice of lemon if desired.

Enjoy your homemade limoncello sorbet, with its bright lemon flavor and subtle notes of limoncello liqueur!

Chocolate Hazelnut Gelato

Ingredients:

- 2 cups whole milk
- 1 cup heavy cream
- 3/4 cup granulated sugar
- 1/2 cup Nutella or other chocolate hazelnut spread
- 1/2 cup hazelnuts, toasted and finely chopped (optional)
- 4 large egg yolks
- 1 teaspoon vanilla extract
- Pinch of salt

Instructions:

1. In a medium saucepan, combine the milk, heavy cream, and half of the sugar. Heat over medium heat, stirring occasionally, until the mixture starts to simmer and the sugar is fully dissolved.
2. In a separate bowl, whisk the egg yolks with the remaining sugar until pale and slightly thickened.
3. Slowly pour about 1/2 cup of the warm milk mixture into the egg yolks, whisking constantly to temper the eggs.
4. Gradually pour the tempered egg mixture back into the saucepan with the remaining milk mixture, whisking constantly.
5. Cook the mixture over medium-low heat, stirring constantly with a wooden spoon or spatula, until it thickens slightly and coats the back of the spoon (about 170-175°F or 77-80°C on an instant-read thermometer). Do not let it boil.
6. Remove from heat and stir in the Nutella or chocolate hazelnut spread until well combined. If using, stir in the finely chopped toasted hazelnuts.
7. Stir in the vanilla extract and a pinch of salt.
8. Let the mixture cool to room temperature, then cover the bowl with plastic wrap, pressing it directly onto the surface of the custard to prevent a skin from forming. Refrigerate until completely chilled, preferably overnight.
9. Once chilled, churn the custard in an ice cream maker according to the manufacturer's instructions until it reaches a soft-serve consistency.
10. Transfer the chocolate hazelnut gelato to an airtight container and freeze for at least 2 hours or until firm before serving.

Enjoy your homemade chocolate hazelnut gelato, with its creamy texture and irresistible chocolate hazelnut flavor!

Bacio Gelato (Chocolate and Hazelnut)

Ingredients:

- 2 cups whole milk
- 1 cup heavy cream
- 3/4 cup granulated sugar
- 4 ounces dark chocolate, finely chopped
- 1/2 cup hazelnuts, toasted and finely chopped
- 4 large egg yolks
- 1 teaspoon vanilla extract
- Pinch of salt

Instructions:

1. In a medium saucepan, combine the milk, heavy cream, and half of the sugar. Heat over medium heat, stirring occasionally, until the mixture starts to simmer and the sugar is fully dissolved.
2. Remove the saucepan from heat and add the finely chopped dark chocolate. Stir until the chocolate is completely melted and the mixture is smooth. Set aside.
3. In a separate bowl, whisk the egg yolks with the remaining sugar until pale and slightly thickened.
4. Slowly pour about 1/2 cup of the warm chocolate-milk mixture into the egg yolks, whisking constantly to temper the eggs.
5. Gradually pour the tempered egg mixture back into the saucepan with the remaining chocolate-milk mixture, whisking constantly.
6. Cook the mixture over medium-low heat, stirring constantly with a wooden spoon or spatula, until it thickens slightly and coats the back of the spoon (about 170-175°F or 77-80°C on an instant-read thermometer). Do not let it boil.
7. Remove from heat and stir in the vanilla extract and a pinch of salt.
8. Let the mixture cool to room temperature, then cover the bowl with plastic wrap, pressing it directly onto the surface of the custard to prevent a skin from forming. Refrigerate until completely chilled, preferably overnight.
9. Once chilled, churn the custard in an ice cream maker according to the manufacturer's instructions until it reaches a soft-serve consistency.
10. During the last few minutes of churning, add the finely chopped toasted hazelnuts to the gelato mixture, allowing them to mix evenly.
11. Transfer the Bacio gelato to an airtight container and freeze for at least 2 hours or until firm before serving.

Enjoy your homemade Bacio gelato, with its luxurious blend of chocolate and hazelnut flavors, reminiscent of the beloved Italian treat!

Fior di Latte Gelato

Ingredients:

- 2 cups whole milk
- 1 cup heavy cream
- 3/4 cup granulated sugar
- 4 large egg yolks
- 1 teaspoon vanilla extract
- Pinch of salt

Instructions:

1. In a medium saucepan, combine the whole milk, heavy cream, and half of the sugar. Heat over medium heat, stirring occasionally, until the mixture begins to simmer and the sugar is completely dissolved.
2. In a separate bowl, whisk together the egg yolks and the remaining sugar until pale and slightly thickened.
3. Slowly pour about 1/2 cup of the warm milk mixture into the egg yolks, whisking constantly to temper the eggs.
4. Gradually pour the tempered egg mixture back into the saucepan with the remaining milk mixture, whisking constantly.
5. Cook the mixture over medium-low heat, stirring constantly with a wooden spoon or spatula, until it thickens slightly and coats the back of the spoon (about 170-175°F or 77-80°C on an instant-read thermometer). Do not let it boil.
6. Remove the saucepan from heat and stir in the vanilla extract and a pinch of salt.
7. Let the mixture cool to room temperature. Then cover the bowl with plastic wrap, pressing it directly onto the surface of the custard to prevent a skin from forming. Refrigerate until completely chilled, preferably overnight.
8. Once chilled, churn the custard in an ice cream maker according to the manufacturer's instructions until it reaches a soft-serve consistency.
9. Transfer the Fior di latte gelato to an airtight container and freeze for at least 2 hours or until firm before serving.
10. Serve the Fior di latte gelato in chilled bowls or cones. You can also garnish it with fresh fruits or a drizzle of honey, if desired.

Enjoy your homemade Fior di latte gelato, with its smooth and creamy milk flavor that's perfect on its own or paired with other desserts!

Cioccolato Gelato

Ingredients:

- 2 cups whole milk
- 1 cup heavy cream
- 3/4 cup granulated sugar
- 4 ounces dark chocolate, finely chopped
- 1/4 cup unsweetened cocoa powder
- 4 large egg yolks
- 1 teaspoon vanilla extract
- Pinch of salt

Instructions:

1. In a medium saucepan, combine the whole milk, heavy cream, and half of the sugar. Heat over medium heat, stirring occasionally, until the mixture begins to simmer and the sugar is completely dissolved.
2. Remove the saucepan from heat and add the finely chopped dark chocolate and cocoa powder. Stir until the chocolate and cocoa powder are completely melted and the mixture is smooth. Set aside.
3. In a separate bowl, whisk together the egg yolks and the remaining sugar until pale and slightly thickened.
4. Slowly pour about 1/2 cup of the warm chocolate-milk mixture into the egg yolks, whisking constantly to temper the eggs.
5. Gradually pour the tempered egg mixture back into the saucepan with the remaining chocolate-milk mixture, whisking constantly.
6. Cook the mixture over medium-low heat, stirring constantly with a wooden spoon or spatula, until it thickens slightly and coats the back of the spoon (about 170-175°F or 77-80°C on an instant-read thermometer). Do not let it boil.
7. Remove from heat and stir in the vanilla extract and a pinch of salt.
8. Let the mixture cool to room temperature, then cover the bowl with plastic wrap, pressing it directly onto the surface of the custard to prevent a skin from forming. Refrigerate until completely chilled, preferably overnight.
9. Once chilled, churn the custard in an ice cream maker according to the manufacturer's instructions until it reaches a soft-serve consistency.
10. Transfer the cioccolato gelato to an airtight container and freeze for at least 2 hours or until firm before serving.
11. Serve the cioccolato gelato in chilled bowls or cones. You can also garnish it with chocolate shavings or a sprinkle of cocoa powder for an extra chocolatey touch.

Enjoy your homemade cioccolato gelato, with its decadent chocolate flavor and creamy texture that's perfect for any chocolate lover!

Cappuccino Gelato

Ingredients:

- 2 cups whole milk
- 1 cup heavy cream
- 3/4 cup granulated sugar
- 1/2 cup brewed espresso or strong coffee, cooled
- 4 large egg yolks
- 1 teaspoon vanilla extract
- Pinch of salt

Instructions:

1. In a medium saucepan, combine the whole milk, heavy cream, and half of the sugar. Heat over medium heat, stirring occasionally, until the mixture begins to simmer and the sugar is completely dissolved.
2. Remove the saucepan from heat and stir in the brewed espresso or strong coffee. Mix until well combined. Set aside.
3. In a separate bowl, whisk together the egg yolks and the remaining sugar until pale and slightly thickened.
4. Slowly pour about 1/2 cup of the warm milk-coffee mixture into the egg yolks, whisking constantly to temper the eggs.
5. Gradually pour the tempered egg mixture back into the saucepan with the remaining milk-coffee mixture, whisking constantly.
6. Cook the mixture over medium-low heat, stirring constantly with a wooden spoon or spatula, until it thickens slightly and coats the back of the spoon (about 170-175°F or 77-80°C on an instant-read thermometer). Do not let it boil.
7. Remove from heat and stir in the vanilla extract and a pinch of salt.
8. Let the mixture cool to room temperature, then cover the bowl with plastic wrap, pressing it directly onto the surface of the custard to prevent a skin from forming. Refrigerate until completely chilled, preferably overnight.
9. Once chilled, churn the custard in an ice cream maker according to the manufacturer's instructions until it reaches a soft-serve consistency.
10. Transfer the cappuccino gelato to an airtight container and freeze for at least 2 hours or until firm before serving.
11. Serve the cappuccino gelato in chilled bowls or cones, garnished with a dusting of cocoa powder or chocolate-covered coffee beans if desired.

Enjoy your homemade cappuccino gelato, with its smooth coffee flavor and creamy texture that's perfect for coffee enthusiasts!

Salted Caramel Gelato

Ingredients:

- 2 cups whole milk
- 1 cup heavy cream
- 1 cup granulated sugar, divided
- 4 large egg yolks
- 1 teaspoon vanilla extract
- 1/2 cup caramel sauce (homemade or store-bought)
- 1 teaspoon flaky sea salt (such as Maldon), plus more for garnish

Instructions:

1. In a medium saucepan, combine the whole milk, heavy cream, and 1/2 cup of granulated sugar. Heat over medium heat, stirring occasionally, until the mixture starts to simmer and the sugar is completely dissolved.
2. In a separate bowl, whisk together the egg yolks and the remaining 1/2 cup of granulated sugar until pale and slightly thickened.
3. Slowly pour about 1/2 cup of the warm milk-cream mixture into the egg yolks, whisking constantly to temper the eggs.
4. Gradually pour the tempered egg mixture back into the saucepan with the remaining milk-cream mixture, whisking constantly.
5. Cook the mixture over medium-low heat, stirring constantly with a wooden spoon or spatula, until it thickens slightly and coats the back of the spoon (about 170-175°F or 77-80°C on an instant-read thermometer). Do not let it boil.
6. Remove from heat and stir in the vanilla extract, caramel sauce, and flaky sea salt. Mix until well combined.
7. Let the mixture cool to room temperature, then cover the bowl with plastic wrap, pressing it directly onto the surface of the custard to prevent a skin from forming. Refrigerate until completely chilled, preferably overnight.
8. Once chilled, churn the custard in an ice cream maker according to the manufacturer's instructions until it reaches a soft-serve consistency.
9. Transfer the salted caramel gelato to an airtight container and freeze for at least 2 hours or until firm before serving.
10. Serve the salted caramel gelato in chilled bowls or cones, sprinkled with a bit more flaky sea salt for garnish if desired.

Enjoy your homemade salted caramel gelato, with its creamy texture and delightful balance of sweet caramel and salty undertones!

Coconut Gelato

Ingredients:

- 2 cups coconut milk (full-fat)
- 1 cup whole milk
- 1 cup heavy cream
- 3/4 cup granulated sugar
- 4 large egg yolks
- 1 teaspoon vanilla extract
- 1 cup shredded coconut (sweetened or unsweetened), toasted (optional)

Instructions:

1. In a medium saucepan, combine the coconut milk, whole milk, heavy cream, and half of the sugar. Heat over medium heat, stirring occasionally, until the mixture starts to simmer and the sugar is completely dissolved.
2. In a separate bowl, whisk together the egg yolks and the remaining sugar until pale and slightly thickened.
3. Slowly pour about 1/2 cup of the warm coconut milk mixture into the egg yolks, whisking constantly to temper the eggs.
4. Gradually pour the tempered egg mixture back into the saucepan with the remaining coconut milk mixture, whisking constantly.
5. Cook the mixture over medium-low heat, stirring constantly with a wooden spoon or spatula, until it thickens slightly and coats the back of the spoon (about 170-175°F or 77-80°C on an instant-read thermometer). Do not let it boil.
6. Remove from heat and stir in the vanilla extract.
7. If using toasted shredded coconut, stir it into the mixture.
8. Let the mixture cool to room temperature, then cover the bowl with plastic wrap, pressing it directly onto the surface of the custard to prevent a skin from forming. Refrigerate until completely chilled, preferably overnight.
9. Once chilled, churn the custard in an ice cream maker according to the manufacturer's instructions until it reaches a soft-serve consistency.
10. Transfer the coconut gelato to an airtight container and freeze for at least 2 hours or until firm before serving.
11. Serve the coconut gelato in chilled bowls or cones, garnished with toasted shredded coconut on top if desired.

Enjoy your homemade coconut gelato, with its creamy texture and delightful coconut flavor!

Almond Gelato

Ingredients:

- 2 cups whole milk
- 1 cup heavy cream
- 3/4 cup granulated sugar
- 1 cup almond paste or almond butter
- 4 large egg yolks
- 1 teaspoon almond extract
- 1/2 cup sliced almonds, toasted (optional)

Instructions:

1. In a medium saucepan, combine the whole milk, heavy cream, and half of the sugar. Heat over medium heat, stirring occasionally, until the mixture starts to simmer and the sugar is completely dissolved.
2. In a separate bowl, whisk together the egg yolks and the remaining sugar until pale and slightly thickened.
3. Slowly pour about 1/2 cup of the warm milk-cream mixture into the egg yolks, whisking constantly to temper the eggs.
4. Gradually pour the tempered egg mixture back into the saucepan with the remaining milk-cream mixture, whisking constantly.
5. Cook the mixture over medium-low heat, stirring constantly with a wooden spoon or spatula, until it thickens slightly and coats the back of the spoon (about 170-175°F or 77-80°C on an instant-read thermometer). Do not let it boil.
6. Remove from heat and stir in the almond paste or almond butter until well combined. If using almond extract, stir it in as well.
7. Let the mixture cool to room temperature, then cover the bowl with plastic wrap, pressing it directly onto the surface of the custard to prevent a skin from forming. Refrigerate until completely chilled, preferably overnight.
8. Once chilled, churn the custard in an ice cream maker according to the manufacturer's instructions until it reaches a soft-serve consistency.
9. During the last few minutes of churning, add the toasted sliced almonds if using, allowing them to mix evenly.
10. Transfer the almond gelato to an airtight container and freeze for at least 2 hours or until firm before serving.
11. Serve the almond gelato in chilled bowls or cones, garnished with additional toasted sliced almonds on top if desired.

Enjoy your homemade almond gelato, with its rich almond flavor and creamy texture!

Cherry Gelato

Ingredients:

- 2 cups whole milk
- 1 cup heavy cream
- 3/4 cup granulated sugar
- 2 cups fresh cherries, pitted and chopped
- 1 tablespoon lemon juice
- 4 large egg yolks
- 1 teaspoon vanilla extract
- Pinch of salt

Instructions:

1. In a medium saucepan, combine the whole milk, heavy cream, and half of the sugar. Heat over medium heat, stirring occasionally, until the mixture starts to simmer and the sugar is completely dissolved.
2. In a separate bowl, combine the chopped cherries with the remaining sugar and lemon juice. Let them macerate for about 15-20 minutes to release their juices.
3. Transfer the cherry mixture to a blender or food processor and blend until smooth. Strain through a fine-mesh sieve to remove any solids, pressing with a spoon to extract as much liquid as possible.
4. In a separate bowl, whisk together the egg yolks until pale and slightly thickened.
5. Slowly pour about 1/2 cup of the warm milk-cream mixture into the egg yolks, whisking constantly to temper the eggs.
6. Gradually pour the tempered egg mixture back into the saucepan with the remaining milk-cream mixture, whisking constantly.
7. Cook the mixture over medium-low heat, stirring constantly with a wooden spoon or spatula, until it thickens slightly and coats the back of the spoon (about 170-175°F or 77-80°C on an instant-read thermometer). Do not let it boil.
8. Remove from heat and stir in the vanilla extract and a pinch of salt.
9. Let the mixture cool to room temperature, then cover the bowl with plastic wrap, pressing it directly onto the surface of the custard to prevent a skin from forming. Refrigerate until completely chilled, preferably overnight.
10. Once chilled, churn the custard in an ice cream maker according to the manufacturer's instructions until it reaches a soft-serve consistency.
11. Transfer the cherry gelato to an airtight container and freeze for at least 2 hours or until firm before serving.

12. Serve the cherry gelato in chilled bowls or cones, garnished with fresh cherry slices or a drizzle of cherry syrup if desired.

Enjoy your homemade cherry gelato, with its vibrant cherry flavor and creamy texture!

Watermelon Sorbet

Ingredients:

- 4 cups seedless watermelon cubes (about 1 small watermelon)
- 1/2 cup granulated sugar
- 1/4 cup freshly squeezed lemon juice
- Zest of 1 lemon (optional)
- 1/4 cup water (optional, if needed for blending)

Instructions:

1. Cut the watermelon into cubes, discarding any seeds.
2. In a blender or food processor, combine the watermelon cubes, granulated sugar, lemon juice, and optional lemon zest.
3. Blend until smooth. If the mixture is too thick to blend smoothly, add a little water, 1 tablespoon at a time, until the mixture blends easily.
4. Taste the mixture and adjust sweetness by adding more sugar if desired, blending again until sugar is dissolved.
5. Pour the watermelon mixture through a fine-mesh sieve into a bowl to remove any pulp or fibers. This step is optional if you prefer a smoother sorbet.
6. Transfer the strained mixture into an ice cream maker and churn according to the manufacturer's instructions until it reaches a slushy, sorbet-like consistency. This usually takes about 20-25 minutes.
7. If you don't have an ice cream maker, you can pour the mixture into a shallow dish and place it in the freezer. Every 30 minutes, stir the mixture with a fork to break up ice crystals, repeating until the sorbet is firm but scoopable.
8. Once churned or frozen to desired consistency, transfer the watermelon sorbet to an airtight container and freeze for at least 2 hours before serving to firm up.
9. Serve the watermelon sorbet in chilled bowls or cones. Garnish with fresh mint leaves or a slice of watermelon for presentation, if desired.

Enjoy your homemade watermelon sorbet, with its light and refreshing taste that's perfect for cooling down on a hot day!

Pineapple Sorbet

Ingredients:

- 1 ripe pineapple, peeled, cored, and cut into chunks (about 4 cups)
- 1/2 cup granulated sugar
- 1/4 cup water
- 2 tablespoons freshly squeezed lemon juice
- Pinch of salt

Instructions:

1. In a small saucepan, combine the granulated sugar and water. Heat over medium heat, stirring occasionally, until the sugar is completely dissolved. Remove from heat and let the simple syrup cool to room temperature.
2. In a blender or food processor, combine the pineapple chunks, cooled simple syrup, lemon juice, and a pinch of salt.
3. Blend the mixture until smooth and well combined. Taste and adjust sweetness or tartness by adding more sugar or lemon juice if desired.
4. Pour the pineapple mixture through a fine-mesh sieve into a bowl to remove any pulp or fibers, if desired for a smoother sorbet texture.
5. Transfer the strained mixture into an ice cream maker and churn according to the manufacturer's instructions until it reaches a slushy, sorbet-like consistency. This usually takes about 20-25 minutes.
6. If you don't have an ice cream maker, pour the pineapple mixture into a shallow dish and place it in the freezer. Every 30 minutes, stir the mixture with a fork to break up ice crystals, repeating until the sorbet is firm but scoopable.
7. Once churned or frozen to desired consistency, transfer the pineapple sorbet to an airtight container and freeze for at least 2 hours before serving to firm up.
8. Serve the pineapple sorbet in chilled bowls or cones. Garnish with a slice of pineapple or a sprig of mint for presentation, if desired.

Enjoy your homemade pineapple sorbet, with its bright and tropical flavor that's perfect for a refreshing treat!

Kiwi Sorbet

Ingredients:

- 6 ripe kiwi fruits, peeled and chopped (about 2 cups)
- 1/2 cup granulated sugar
- 1/4 cup water
- 2 tablespoons freshly squeezed lemon juice
- Pinch of salt

Instructions:

1. In a small saucepan, combine the granulated sugar and water. Heat over medium heat, stirring occasionally, until the sugar is completely dissolved. Remove from heat and let the simple syrup cool to room temperature.
2. In a blender or food processor, combine the chopped kiwi fruits, cooled simple syrup, lemon juice, and a pinch of salt.
3. Blend the mixture until smooth and well combined. Taste and adjust sweetness or tartness by adding more sugar or lemon juice if desired.
4. Pour the kiwi mixture through a fine-mesh sieve into a bowl to remove any seeds or pulp for a smoother sorbet texture.
5. Transfer the strained mixture into an ice cream maker and churn according to the manufacturer's instructions until it reaches a slushy, sorbet-like consistency. This typically takes about 20-25 minutes.
6. If you don't have an ice cream maker, pour the kiwi mixture into a shallow dish and place it in the freezer. Every 30 minutes, stir the mixture with a fork to break up ice crystals, repeating until the sorbet is firm but scoopable.
7. Once churned or frozen to your desired consistency, transfer the kiwi sorbet to an airtight container and freeze for at least 2 hours before serving to firm up.
8. Serve the kiwi sorbet in chilled bowls or cones. Garnish with a slice of kiwi or a sprig of mint for presentation, if desired.

Enjoy your homemade kiwi sorbet, with its refreshing and tangy flavor that's perfect for a light and delightful dessert!

Passion Fruit Sorbet

Ingredients:

- 1 cup passion fruit pulp (about 6-8 passion fruits)
- 1 cup water
- 3/4 cup granulated sugar
- 2 tablespoons freshly squeezed lemon juice

Instructions:

1. Cut the passion fruits in half and scoop out the pulp into a blender or food processor.
2. Add the water to the blender with the passion fruit pulp. Blend until smooth.
3. Pour the blended mixture through a fine-mesh sieve into a bowl to remove any seeds or pulp, pressing with a spoon to extract as much liquid as possible.
4. In a small saucepan, combine the sugar and 1/2 cup of water. Heat over medium heat, stirring occasionally, until the sugar is completely dissolved to make a simple syrup. Remove from heat and let it cool to room temperature.
5. Add the cooled simple syrup and freshly squeezed lemon juice to the passion fruit puree. Stir well to combine.
6. Taste the mixture and adjust sweetness or tartness by adding more sugar or lemon juice if desired.
7. Transfer the passion fruit mixture into an ice cream maker and churn according to the manufacturer's instructions until it reaches a slushy, sorbet-like consistency. This typically takes about 20-25 minutes.
8. If you don't have an ice cream maker, pour the passion fruit mixture into a shallow dish and place it in the freezer. Every 30 minutes, stir the mixture with a fork to break up ice crystals, repeating until the sorbet is firm but scoopable.
9. Once churned or frozen to your desired consistency, transfer the passion fruit sorbet to an airtight container and freeze for at least 2 hours before serving to firm up.
10. Serve the passion fruit sorbet in chilled bowls or cones. Garnish with a slice of passion fruit or a sprig of mint for presentation, if desired.

Enjoy your homemade passion fruit sorbet, with its tropical and tangy flavor that's perfect for a refreshing and exotic dessert!

Melon Sorbet

Ingredients:

- 4 cups cubed melon (such as cantaloupe, honeydew, or watermelon)
- 1/2 cup granulated sugar
- 1/4 cup water
- 2 tablespoons freshly squeezed lemon juice
- Pinch of salt

Instructions:

1. In a small saucepan, combine the granulated sugar and water. Heat over medium heat, stirring occasionally, until the sugar is completely dissolved. Remove from heat and let the simple syrup cool to room temperature.
2. In a blender or food processor, puree the cubed melon until smooth.
3. Pour the melon puree through a fine-mesh sieve into a bowl to remove any seeds or pulp, pressing with a spoon to extract as much liquid as possible.
4. Stir in the cooled simple syrup, freshly squeezed lemon juice, and a pinch of salt into the melon puree. Mix well to combine.
5. Taste the mixture and adjust sweetness or tartness by adding more sugar or lemon juice if desired.
6. Transfer the melon mixture into an ice cream maker and churn according to the manufacturer's instructions until it reaches a slushy, sorbet-like consistency. This typically takes about 20-25 minutes.
7. If you don't have an ice cream maker, pour the melon mixture into a shallow dish and place it in the freezer. Every 30 minutes, stir the mixture with a fork to break up ice crystals, repeating until the sorbet is firm but scoopable.
8. Once churned or frozen to your desired consistency, transfer the melon sorbet to an airtight container and freeze for at least 2 hours before serving to firm up.
9. Serve the melon sorbet in chilled bowls or cones. Garnish with a slice of melon or a sprig of mint for presentation, if desired.

Enjoy your homemade melon sorbet, with its fresh and fruity flavor that's perfect for a light and refreshing dessert!

White Peach Sorbet

Ingredients:

- 4 cups ripe white peaches, peeled and diced (about 6-8 peaches)
- 1/2 cup granulated sugar
- 1/4 cup water
- 2 tablespoons freshly squeezed lemon juice
- Pinch of salt

Instructions:

1. In a small saucepan, combine the granulated sugar and water. Heat over medium heat, stirring occasionally, until the sugar is completely dissolved. Remove from heat and let the simple syrup cool to room temperature.
2. In a blender or food processor, puree the diced white peaches until smooth.
3. Pour the peach puree through a fine-mesh sieve into a bowl to remove any fibers or solids, pressing with a spoon to extract as much liquid as possible.
4. Stir in the cooled simple syrup, freshly squeezed lemon juice, and a pinch of salt into the peach puree. Mix well to combine.
5. Taste the mixture and adjust sweetness or tartness by adding more sugar or lemon juice if desired.
6. Transfer the peach mixture into an ice cream maker and churn according to the manufacturer's instructions until it reaches a slushy, sorbet-like consistency. This typically takes about 20-25 minutes.
7. If you don't have an ice cream maker, pour the peach mixture into a shallow dish and place it in the freezer. Every 30 minutes, stir the mixture with a fork to break up ice crystals, repeating until the sorbet is firm but scoopable.
8. Once churned or frozen to your desired consistency, transfer the white peach sorbet to an airtight container and freeze for at least 2 hours before serving to firm up.
9. Serve the white peach sorbet in chilled bowls or cones. Garnish with a slice of white peach or a sprig of mint for presentation, if desired.

Enjoy your homemade white peach sorbet, with its delicate flavor and smooth texture that's perfect for a refreshing summer treat!

Pear Sorbet

Ingredients:

- 4 ripe pears, peeled, cored, and diced (about 4 cups)
- 1/2 cup granulated sugar
- 1/4 cup water
- 2 tablespoons freshly squeezed lemon juice
- Pinch of salt

Instructions:

1. In a small saucepan, combine the granulated sugar and water. Heat over medium heat, stirring occasionally, until the sugar is completely dissolved. Remove from heat and let the simple syrup cool to room temperature.
2. In a blender or food processor, puree the diced pears until smooth.
3. Pour the pear puree through a fine-mesh sieve into a bowl to remove any fibers or solids, pressing with a spoon to extract as much liquid as possible.
4. Stir in the cooled simple syrup, freshly squeezed lemon juice, and a pinch of salt into the pear puree. Mix well to combine.
5. Taste the mixture and adjust sweetness or tartness by adding more sugar or lemon juice if desired.
6. Transfer the pear mixture into an ice cream maker and churn according to the manufacturer's instructions until it reaches a slushy, sorbet-like consistency. This typically takes about 20-25 minutes.
7. If you don't have an ice cream maker, pour the pear mixture into a shallow dish and place it in the freezer. Every 30 minutes, stir the mixture with a fork to break up ice crystals, repeating until the sorbet is firm but scoopable.
8. Once churned or frozen to your desired consistency, transfer the pear sorbet to an airtight container and freeze for at least 2 hours before serving to firm up.
9. Serve the pear sorbet in chilled bowls or cones. Garnish with a slice of pear or a sprig of mint for presentation, if desired.

Enjoy your homemade pear sorbet, with its natural sweetness and smooth texture that's perfect for a light and refreshing dessert!

Fig Gelato

Ingredients:

- 1 pound fresh figs, stemmed and quartered (about 3 cups)
- 1 cup whole milk
- 1 cup heavy cream
- 3/4 cup granulated sugar
- 4 large egg yolks
- 1 teaspoon vanilla extract
- Pinch of salt

Instructions:

1. In a medium saucepan, combine the whole milk, heavy cream, and half of the sugar. Heat over medium heat, stirring occasionally, until the mixture starts to simmer and the sugar is completely dissolved.
2. Add the quartered figs to the milk-cream mixture. Simmer gently for about 5-7 minutes, until the figs are softened.
3. Remove the saucepan from heat and let the mixture cool slightly. Transfer the fig mixture to a blender or food processor and blend until smooth.
4. Pour the blended fig mixture through a fine-mesh sieve into a bowl to remove any seeds or large pieces of skin, pressing with a spoon to extract as much liquid as possible. Discard solids.
5. In a separate bowl, whisk together the egg yolks and the remaining sugar until pale and slightly thickened.
6. Slowly pour about 1/2 cup of the warm fig-infused milk-cream mixture into the egg yolks, whisking constantly to temper the eggs.
7. Gradually pour the tempered egg mixture back into the saucepan with the remaining milk-cream mixture, whisking constantly.
8. Cook the mixture over medium-low heat, stirring constantly with a wooden spoon or spatula, until it thickens slightly and coats the back of the spoon (about 170-175°F or 77-80°C on an instant-read thermometer). Do not let it boil.
9. Remove from heat and stir in the vanilla extract and a pinch of salt.
10. Let the mixture cool to room temperature, then cover the bowl with plastic wrap, pressing it directly onto the surface of the custard to prevent a skin from forming. Refrigerate until completely chilled, preferably overnight.
11. Once chilled, churn the fig custard in an ice cream maker according to the manufacturer's instructions until it reaches a soft-serve consistency.

12. Transfer the fig gelato to an airtight container and freeze for at least 2 hours or until firm before serving.
13. Serve the fig gelato in chilled bowls or cones. Garnish with fresh fig slices or a drizzle of honey for presentation, if desired.

Enjoy your homemade fig gelato, with its rich fig flavor and creamy texture that's perfect for a unique and delicious dessert!

Walnut Gelato

Ingredients:

- 1 cup shelled walnuts
- 2 cups whole milk
- 1 cup heavy cream
- 3/4 cup granulated sugar
- 4 large egg yolks
- 1 teaspoon vanilla extract
- Pinch of salt

Instructions:

1. Preheat your oven to 350°F (175°C). Spread the walnuts evenly on a baking sheet and toast them in the oven for about 8-10 minutes, or until lightly browned and fragrant. Remove from the oven and let them cool.
2. In a medium saucepan, combine the whole milk, heavy cream, and half of the sugar. Heat over medium heat, stirring occasionally, until the mixture starts to simmer and the sugar is completely dissolved.
3. In a blender or food processor, grind the toasted walnuts until finely chopped.
4. Add the ground walnuts to the milk-cream mixture in the saucepan. Simmer gently for about 5 minutes to infuse the flavors, stirring occasionally.
5. Remove the saucepan from heat and let the walnut-infused mixture cool slightly. Strain the mixture through a fine-mesh sieve into a bowl to remove the walnut pieces, pressing with a spoon to extract as much liquid as possible.
6. In a separate bowl, whisk together the egg yolks and the remaining sugar until pale and slightly thickened.
7. Slowly pour about 1/2 cup of the warm walnut-infused milk-cream mixture into the egg yolks, whisking constantly to temper the eggs.
8. Gradually pour the tempered egg mixture back into the saucepan with the remaining milk-cream mixture, whisking constantly.
9. Cook the mixture over medium-low heat, stirring constantly with a wooden spoon or spatula, until it thickens slightly and coats the back of the spoon (about 170-175°F or 77-80°C on an instant-read thermometer). Do not let it boil.
10. Remove from heat and stir in the vanilla extract and a pinch of salt.
11. Let the mixture cool to room temperature, then cover the bowl with plastic wrap, pressing it directly onto the surface of the custard to prevent a skin from forming. Refrigerate until completely chilled, preferably overnight.

12. Once chilled, churn the walnut custard in an ice cream maker according to the manufacturer's instructions until it reaches a soft-serve consistency.
13. Transfer the walnut gelato to an airtight container and freeze for at least 2 hours or until firm before serving.
14. Serve the walnut gelato in chilled bowls or cones. Garnish with chopped toasted walnuts or a drizzle of honey for presentation, if desired.

Enjoy your homemade walnut gelato, with its rich walnut flavor and creamy texture that's perfect for a decadent dessert!

Biscotti Gelato

Ingredients:

- 2 cups whole milk
- 1 cup heavy cream
- 3/4 cup granulated sugar
- 4 large egg yolks
- 1 teaspoon vanilla extract
- Pinch of salt
- 1 cup crushed biscotti (your favorite flavor, such as almond, chocolate chip, or hazelnut)

Instructions:

1. In a medium saucepan, combine the whole milk, heavy cream, and half of the sugar. Heat over medium heat, stirring occasionally, until the mixture starts to simmer and the sugar is completely dissolved.
2. In a separate bowl, whisk together the egg yolks and the remaining sugar until pale and slightly thickened.
3. Slowly pour about 1/2 cup of the warm milk-cream mixture into the egg yolks, whisking constantly to temper the eggs.
4. Gradually pour the tempered egg mixture back into the saucepan with the remaining milk-cream mixture, whisking constantly.
5. Cook the mixture over medium-low heat, stirring constantly with a wooden spoon or spatula, until it thickens slightly and coats the back of the spoon (about 170-175°F or 77-80°C on an instant-read thermometer). Do not let it boil.
6. Remove from heat and stir in the vanilla extract and a pinch of salt.
7. Let the mixture cool to room temperature, then cover the bowl with plastic wrap, pressing it directly onto the surface of the custard to prevent a skin from forming. Refrigerate until completely chilled, preferably overnight.
8. Once chilled, churn the custard in an ice cream maker according to the manufacturer's instructions until it reaches a soft-serve consistency.
9. During the last few minutes of churning, add the crushed biscotti to the ice cream maker and let it incorporate into the gelato.
10. Transfer the biscotti gelato to an airtight container and freeze for at least 2 hours or until firm before serving.
11. Serve the biscotti gelato in chilled bowls or cones. You can garnish with additional crushed biscotti on top for extra texture and flavor.

Enjoy your homemade biscotti gelato, with its creamy base and crunchy biscotti pieces, creating a delightful Italian dessert experience!

Marsala Gelato

Ingredients:

- 2 cups whole milk
- 1 cup heavy cream
- 3/4 cup granulated sugar
- 4 large egg yolks
- 1/2 cup Marsala wine
- 1 teaspoon vanilla extract
- Pinch of salt

Instructions:

1. In a medium saucepan, combine the whole milk, heavy cream, and half of the sugar. Heat over medium heat, stirring occasionally, until the mixture starts to simmer and the sugar is completely dissolved.
2. In a separate bowl, whisk together the egg yolks and the remaining sugar until pale and slightly thickened.
3. Slowly pour about 1/2 cup of the warm milk-cream mixture into the egg yolks, whisking constantly to temper the eggs.
4. Gradually pour the tempered egg mixture back into the saucepan with the remaining milk-cream mixture, whisking constantly.
5. Cook the mixture over medium-low heat, stirring constantly with a wooden spoon or spatula, until it thickens slightly and coats the back of the spoon (about 170-175°F or 77-80°C on an instant-read thermometer). Do not let it boil.
6. Remove from heat and stir in the Marsala wine, vanilla extract, and a pinch of salt.
7. Let the mixture cool to room temperature, then cover the bowl with plastic wrap, pressing it directly onto the surface of the custard to prevent a skin from forming. Refrigerate until completely chilled, preferably overnight.
8. Once chilled, churn the Marsala custard in an ice cream maker according to the manufacturer's instructions until it reaches a soft-serve consistency.
9. Transfer the Marsala gelato to an airtight container and freeze for at least 2 hours or until firm before serving.
10. Serve the Marsala gelato in chilled bowls or cones. You can garnish with a sprinkle of cocoa powder or shaved chocolate for presentation, if desired.

Enjoy your homemade Marsala gelato, with its unique wine-infused flavor and creamy texture that's perfect for a sophisticated dessert!

Panna Cotta Gelato

Ingredients:

- 2 cups whole milk
- 1 cup heavy cream
- 1/2 cup granulated sugar
- 1 vanilla bean, split lengthwise (or 1 teaspoon vanilla extract)
- 4 sheets gelatin (or 1 tablespoon powdered gelatin)
- 1/4 cup cold water
- Pinch of salt

Instructions:

1. In a medium saucepan, combine the whole milk, heavy cream, and granulated sugar. If using a vanilla bean, scrape the seeds into the mixture and add the pod as well. Heat over medium-low heat, stirring occasionally, until the mixture starts to simmer and the sugar is completely dissolved. If using vanilla extract, add it after the mixture is heated.
2. While the milk mixture is heating, place the gelatin sheets in a bowl of cold water to soften. If using powdered gelatin, sprinkle it over the cold water in a small bowl and let it bloom for 5-10 minutes.
3. Once the milk mixture is simmering and the sugar is dissolved, remove from heat and remove the vanilla bean pod if used. Squeeze excess water from the softened gelatin sheets and add them to the hot milk mixture, stirring until completely dissolved. If using powdered gelatin, stir the bloomed gelatin mixture into the hot milk until dissolved.
4. Stir in a pinch of salt. Let the mixture cool to room temperature.
5. Once cooled, strain the mixture through a fine-mesh sieve into a bowl to remove any clumps or solids.
6. Cover the bowl with plastic wrap, pressing it directly onto the surface of the mixture to prevent a skin from forming. Refrigerate until completely chilled, preferably overnight.
7. Once chilled, churn the panna cotta mixture in an ice cream maker according to the manufacturer's instructions until it reaches a soft-serve consistency.
8. Transfer the churned panna cotta gelato to an airtight container and freeze for at least 2 hours or until firm before serving.
9. Serve the panna cotta gelato in chilled bowls or cones. You can garnish with fresh berries, a drizzle of caramel or berry sauce, or grated chocolate for presentation, if desired.

Enjoy your homemade panna cotta gelato, with its creamy texture and delicate vanilla flavor, perfect for a luxurious dessert experience!

Ricotta Gelato

Ingredients:

- 2 cups whole milk
- 1 cup heavy cream
- 1 cup ricotta cheese (preferably whole milk ricotta)
- 3/4 cup granulated sugar
- 4 large egg yolks
- 1 teaspoon vanilla extract
- Pinch of salt

Instructions:

1. In a medium saucepan, combine the whole milk, heavy cream, and half of the sugar. Heat over medium heat, stirring occasionally, until the mixture starts to simmer and the sugar is completely dissolved.
2. In a separate bowl, whisk together the egg yolks and the remaining sugar until pale and slightly thickened.
3. Slowly pour about 1/2 cup of the warm milk-cream mixture into the egg yolks, whisking constantly to temper the eggs.
4. Gradually pour the tempered egg mixture back into the saucepan with the remaining milk-cream mixture, whisking constantly.
5. Cook the mixture over medium-low heat, stirring constantly with a wooden spoon or spatula, until it thickens slightly and coats the back of the spoon (about 170-175°F or 77-80°C on an instant-read thermometer). Do not let it boil.
6. Remove from heat and whisk in the ricotta cheese until smooth and well combined.
7. Stir in the vanilla extract and a pinch of salt.
8. Let the mixture cool to room temperature, then cover the bowl with plastic wrap, pressing it directly onto the surface of the custard to prevent a skin from forming. Refrigerate until completely chilled, preferably overnight.
9. Once chilled, churn the ricotta custard in an ice cream maker according to the manufacturer's instructions until it reaches a soft-serve consistency.
10. Transfer the ricotta gelato to an airtight container and freeze for at least 2 hours or until firm before serving.
11. Serve the ricotta gelato in chilled bowls or cones. You can garnish with a sprinkle of crushed pistachios, a drizzle of honey, or fresh berries for presentation, if desired.

Enjoy your homemade ricotta gelato, with its creamy texture and delicate ricotta flavor that's perfect for a sophisticated and delicious dessert!

Yogurt Gelato

Ingredients:

- 2 cups whole milk
- 1 cup heavy cream
- 1 cup Greek yogurt (full-fat for creamier texture)
- 3/4 cup granulated sugar
- 4 large egg yolks
- 1 teaspoon vanilla extract
- Pinch of salt

Instructions:

1. In a medium saucepan, combine the whole milk, heavy cream, and half of the sugar. Heat over medium heat, stirring occasionally, until the mixture starts to simmer and the sugar is completely dissolved.
2. In a separate bowl, whisk together the egg yolks and the remaining sugar until pale and slightly thickened.
3. Slowly pour about 1/2 cup of the warm milk-cream mixture into the egg yolks, whisking constantly to temper the eggs.
4. Gradually pour the tempered egg mixture back into the saucepan with the remaining milk-cream mixture, whisking constantly.
5. Cook the mixture over medium-low heat, stirring constantly with a wooden spoon or spatula, until it thickens slightly and coats the back of the spoon (about 170-175°F or 77-80°C on an instant-read thermometer). Do not let it boil.
6. Remove from heat and whisk in the Greek yogurt until smooth and well combined.
7. Stir in the vanilla extract and a pinch of salt.
8. Let the mixture cool to room temperature, then cover the bowl with plastic wrap, pressing it directly onto the surface of the custard to prevent a skin from forming. Refrigerate until completely chilled, preferably overnight.
9. Once chilled, churn the yogurt custard in an ice cream maker according to the manufacturer's instructions until it reaches a soft-serve consistency.
10. Transfer the yogurt gelato to an airtight container and freeze for at least 2 hours or until firm before serving.
11. Serve the yogurt gelato in chilled bowls or cones. You can garnish with fresh berries, a drizzle of honey or maple syrup, or a sprinkle of granola for presentation, if desired.

Enjoy your homemade yogurt gelato, with its creamy texture and tangy yogurt flavor that's perfect for a refreshing and healthier dessert option!

Basil Gelato

Ingredients:

- 2 cups whole milk
- 1 cup heavy cream
- 1 cup fresh basil leaves, washed and dried
- 3/4 cup granulated sugar
- 4 large egg yolks
- Pinch of salt

Instructions:

1. In a medium saucepan, combine the whole milk, heavy cream, and half of the sugar. Heat over medium heat, stirring occasionally, until the mixture starts to simmer and the sugar is completely dissolved.
2. Add the fresh basil leaves to the milk-cream mixture and stir gently. Simmer for about 5 minutes to infuse the basil flavor. Remove from heat and let the mixture cool slightly.
3. In a separate bowl, whisk together the egg yolks and the remaining sugar until pale and slightly thickened.
4. Strain the basil-infused milk-cream mixture through a fine-mesh sieve into a bowl, pressing the basil leaves with a spoon to extract as much flavor as possible. Discard the basil leaves.
5. Slowly pour about 1/2 cup of the warm basil-infused milk-cream mixture into the egg yolks, whisking constantly to temper the eggs.
6. Gradually pour the tempered egg mixture back into the saucepan with the remaining milk-cream mixture, whisking constantly.
7. Cook the mixture over medium-low heat, stirring constantly with a wooden spoon or spatula, until it thickens slightly and coats the back of the spoon (about 170-175°F or 77-80°C on an instant-read thermometer). Do not let it boil.
8. Remove from heat and stir in a pinch of salt.
9. Let the mixture cool to room temperature, then cover the bowl with plastic wrap, pressing it directly onto the surface of the custard to prevent a skin from forming. Refrigerate until completely chilled, preferably overnight.
10. Once chilled, churn the basil custard in an ice cream maker according to the manufacturer's instructions until it reaches a soft-serve consistency.
11. Transfer the basil gelato to an airtight container and freeze for at least 2 hours or until firm before serving.

12. Serve the basil gelato in chilled bowls or cones. You can garnish with a fresh basil leaf or a sprinkle of chopped pistachios for presentation, if desired.

Enjoy your homemade basil gelato, with its unique herbal flavor and creamy texture that's perfect for a refreshing and sophisticated dessert!

Lavender Gelato

Ingredients:

- 2 cups whole milk
- 1 cup heavy cream
- 2 tablespoons dried culinary lavender buds (organic, if possible)
- 3/4 cup granulated sugar
- 4 large egg yolks
- Pinch of salt

Instructions:

1. In a medium saucepan, combine the whole milk, heavy cream, dried lavender buds, and half of the sugar. Heat over medium heat, stirring occasionally, until the mixture just begins to simmer. Do not let it boil.
2. Once simmering, remove the saucepan from heat and cover. Let the lavender steep in the milk-cream mixture for about 15-20 minutes to infuse the flavor. Taste occasionally to ensure the desired lavender flavor is achieved.
3. After steeping, strain the mixture through a fine-mesh sieve into a clean bowl to remove the lavender buds. Press gently with a spoon to extract as much liquid as possible. Discard the lavender buds.
4. In a separate bowl, whisk together the egg yolks and the remaining sugar until pale and slightly thickened.
5. Slowly pour about 1/2 cup of the warm lavender-infused milk-cream mixture into the egg yolks, whisking constantly to temper the eggs.
6. Gradually pour the tempered egg mixture back into the saucepan with the remaining milk-cream mixture, whisking constantly.
7. Cook the mixture over medium-low heat, stirring constantly with a wooden spoon or spatula, until it thickens slightly and coats the back of the spoon (about 170-175°F or 77-80°C on an instant-read thermometer). Do not let it boil.
8. Remove from heat and stir in a pinch of salt.
9. Let the mixture cool to room temperature, then cover the bowl with plastic wrap, pressing it directly onto the surface of the custard to prevent a skin from forming. Refrigerate until completely chilled, preferably overnight.
10. Once chilled, strain the custard through a fine-mesh sieve once more to ensure a smooth texture.
11. Churn the lavender custard in an ice cream maker according to the manufacturer's instructions until it reaches a soft-serve consistency.

12. Transfer the lavender gelato to an airtight container and freeze for at least 2 hours or until firm before serving.
13. Serve the lavender gelato in chilled bowls or cones. You can garnish with a few fresh lavender buds or a drizzle of lavender-infused honey for presentation, if desired.

Enjoy your homemade lavender gelato, with its delicate floral aroma and creamy texture, perfect for a sophisticated and refreshing dessert experience!

Rose Gelato

Ingredients:

- 2 cups whole milk
- 1 cup heavy cream
- 1/4 cup dried rose petals (culinary grade, unsprayed)
- 3/4 cup granulated sugar
- 4 large egg yolks
- 1 teaspoon rose water
- Pinch of salt
- Pink food coloring (optional)

Instructions:

1. In a medium saucepan, combine the whole milk, heavy cream, dried rose petals, and half of the sugar. Heat over medium heat, stirring occasionally, until the mixture just begins to simmer. Do not let it boil.
2. Once simmering, remove the saucepan from heat and cover. Let the rose petals steep in the milk-cream mixture for about 15-20 minutes to infuse the flavor. Taste occasionally to ensure the desired rose flavor is achieved.
3. After steeping, strain the mixture through a fine-mesh sieve into a clean bowl to remove the rose petals. Press gently with a spoon to extract as much liquid as possible. Discard the rose petals.
4. In a separate bowl, whisk together the egg yolks and the remaining sugar until pale and slightly thickened.
5. Slowly pour about 1/2 cup of the warm rose-infused milk-cream mixture into the egg yolks, whisking constantly to temper the eggs.
6. Gradually pour the tempered egg mixture back into the saucepan with the remaining milk-cream mixture, whisking constantly.
7. Cook the mixture over medium-low heat, stirring constantly with a wooden spoon or spatula, until it thickens slightly and coats the back of the spoon (about 170-175°F or 77-80°C on an instant-read thermometer). Do not let it boil.
8. Remove from heat and stir in the rose water and a pinch of salt. Add a few drops of pink food coloring if desired, to achieve a pale pink color.
9. Let the mixture cool to room temperature, then cover the bowl with plastic wrap, pressing it directly onto the surface of the custard to prevent a skin from forming. Refrigerate until completely chilled, preferably overnight.
10. Once chilled, strain the custard through a fine-mesh sieve once more to ensure a smooth texture.

11. Churn the rose custard in an ice cream maker according to the manufacturer's instructions until it reaches a soft-serve consistency.
12. Transfer the rose gelato to an airtight container and freeze for at least 2 hours or until firm before serving.
13. Serve the rose gelato in chilled bowls or cones. You can garnish with a few edible rose petals or a sprinkle of powdered sugar for presentation, if desired.

Enjoy your homemade rose gelato, with its delicate floral aroma and creamy texture, perfect for a sophisticated and refreshing dessert!

Saffron Gelato

Ingredients:

- 2 cups whole milk
- 1 cup heavy cream
- 1/2 teaspoon saffron threads
- 3/4 cup granulated sugar
- 4 large egg yolks
- Pinch of salt

Instructions:

1. In a small bowl, combine the saffron threads with 2 tablespoons of warm milk. Let it steep for about 10-15 minutes to release the color and flavor of the saffron.
2. In a medium saucepan, combine the remaining whole milk, heavy cream, and half of the sugar. Heat over medium heat, stirring occasionally, until the mixture just begins to simmer. Do not let it boil.
3. Once simmering, remove from heat and add the saffron-infused milk (including the saffron threads) to the saucepan. Stir well to combine.
4. In a separate bowl, whisk together the egg yolks and the remaining sugar until pale and slightly thickened.
5. Slowly pour about 1/2 cup of the warm saffron-infused milk-cream mixture into the egg yolks, whisking constantly to temper the eggs.
6. Gradually pour the tempered egg mixture back into the saucepan with the remaining milk-cream mixture, whisking constantly.
7. Cook the mixture over medium-low heat, stirring constantly with a wooden spoon or spatula, until it thickens slightly and coats the back of the spoon (about 170-175°F or 77-80°C on an instant-read thermometer). Do not let it boil.
8. Remove from heat and stir in a pinch of salt.
9. Let the mixture cool to room temperature, then cover the bowl with plastic wrap, pressing it directly onto the surface of the custard to prevent a skin from forming. Refrigerate until completely chilled, preferably overnight.
10. Once chilled, strain the custard through a fine-mesh sieve to remove any solids or saffron threads.
11. Churn the saffron custard in an ice cream maker according to the manufacturer's instructions until it reaches a soft-serve consistency.
12. Transfer the saffron gelato to an airtight container and freeze for at least 2 hours or until firm before serving.

13. Serve the saffron gelato in chilled bowls or cones. You can garnish with a few strands of saffron on top for presentation, if desired.

Enjoy your homemade saffron gelato, with its rich golden color and exotic flavor that's perfect for a special and indulgent dessert!

Mint Gelato

Ingredients:

- 2 cups whole milk
- 1 cup heavy cream
- 1 cup fresh mint leaves, washed and dried
- 3/4 cup granulated sugar
- 4 large egg yolks
- Green food coloring (optional, for enhanced color)
- Pinch of salt

Instructions:

1. In a medium saucepan, combine the whole milk, heavy cream, fresh mint leaves, and half of the sugar. Heat over medium heat, stirring occasionally, until the mixture just begins to simmer. Do not let it boil.
2. Once simmering, remove the saucepan from heat and cover. Let the mint leaves steep in the milk-cream mixture for about 15-20 minutes to infuse the flavor. Taste occasionally to ensure the desired mint flavor is achieved.
3. After steeping, strain the mixture through a fine-mesh sieve into a clean bowl to remove the mint leaves. Press gently with a spoon to extract as much liquid as possible. Discard the mint leaves.
4. In a separate bowl, whisk together the egg yolks and the remaining sugar until pale and slightly thickened.
5. Slowly pour about 1/2 cup of the warm mint-infused milk-cream mixture into the egg yolks, whisking constantly to temper the eggs.
6. Gradually pour the tempered egg mixture back into the saucepan with the remaining milk-cream mixture, whisking constantly.
7. Cook the mixture over medium-low heat, stirring constantly with a wooden spoon or spatula, until it thickens slightly and coats the back of the spoon (about 170-175°F or 77-80°C on an instant-read thermometer). Do not let it boil.
8. Remove from heat and stir in a pinch of salt. Add a few drops of green food coloring if desired, to achieve a vibrant green color.
9. Let the mixture cool to room temperature, then cover the bowl with plastic wrap, pressing it directly onto the surface of the custard to prevent a skin from forming. Refrigerate until completely chilled, preferably overnight.
10. Once chilled, strain the custard through a fine-mesh sieve once more to ensure a smooth texture.

11. Churn the mint custard in an ice cream maker according to the manufacturer's instructions until it reaches a soft-serve consistency.
12. Transfer the mint gelato to an airtight container and freeze for at least 2 hours or until firm before serving.
13. Serve the mint gelato in chilled bowls or cones. You can garnish with a sprig of fresh mint or a sprinkle of chocolate shavings for presentation, if desired.

Enjoy your homemade mint gelato, with its refreshing flavor and creamy texture that's perfect for a delightful dessert experience!

Cardamom Gelato

Ingredients:

- 2 cups whole milk
- 1 cup heavy cream
- 1 tablespoon whole cardamom pods
- 3/4 cup granulated sugar
- 4 large egg yolks
- Pinch of salt

Instructions:

1. In a medium saucepan, combine the whole milk, heavy cream, and whole cardamom pods (lightly crushed with the back of a knife to release flavor). Heat over medium heat, stirring occasionally, until the mixture just begins to simmer. Do not let it boil.
2. Once simmering, remove from heat and cover. Let the cardamom pods steep in the milk-cream mixture for about 15-20 minutes to infuse the flavor. Taste occasionally to ensure the desired cardamom flavor is achieved.
3. After steeping, strain the mixture through a fine-mesh sieve into a clean bowl to remove the cardamom pods. Press gently with a spoon to extract as much liquid as possible. Discard the cardamom pods.
4. In a separate bowl, whisk together the egg yolks and the granulated sugar until pale and slightly thickened.
5. Slowly pour about 1/2 cup of the warm cardamom-infused milk-cream mixture into the egg yolks, whisking constantly to temper the eggs.
6. Gradually pour the tempered egg mixture back into the saucepan with the remaining milk-cream mixture, whisking constantly.
7. Cook the mixture over medium-low heat, stirring constantly with a wooden spoon or spatula, until it thickens slightly and coats the back of the spoon (about 170-175°F or 77-80°C on an instant-read thermometer). Do not let it boil.
8. Remove from heat and stir in a pinch of salt.
9. Let the mixture cool to room temperature, then cover the bowl with plastic wrap, pressing it directly onto the surface of the custard to prevent a skin from forming. Refrigerate until completely chilled, preferably overnight.
10. Once chilled, strain the custard through a fine-mesh sieve once more to ensure a smooth texture.
11. Churn the cardamom custard in an ice cream maker according to the manufacturer's instructions until it reaches a soft-serve consistency.

12. Transfer the cardamom gelato to an airtight container and freeze for at least 2 hours or until firm before serving.
13. Serve the cardamom gelato in chilled bowls or cones. You can garnish with a sprinkle of ground cardamom or chopped pistachios for presentation, if desired.

Enjoy your homemade cardamom gelato, with its aromatic and comforting flavor that's perfect for a unique and delightful dessert experience!

Pistachio Rosewater Gelato

Ingredients:

- 2 cups whole milk
- 1 cup heavy cream
- 3/4 cup granulated sugar
- 1/2 cup shelled pistachios, unsalted
- 4 large egg yolks
- 1 teaspoon rosewater (adjust to taste)
- Pinch of salt
- Green food coloring (optional, for enhanced color)

Instructions:

1. In a blender or food processor, grind the shelled pistachios into a fine powder. You can leave some larger pieces for texture if desired.
2. In a medium saucepan, combine the whole milk, heavy cream, ground pistachios, and half of the sugar. Heat over medium heat, stirring occasionally, until the mixture just begins to simmer. Do not let it boil.
3. Once simmering, remove from heat and cover. Let the pistachios steep in the milk-cream mixture for about 15-20 minutes to infuse the flavor. Stir occasionally to ensure even infusion.
4. After steeping, strain the mixture through a fine-mesh sieve into a clean bowl to remove the ground pistachios. Press gently with a spoon to extract as much liquid as possible. Discard the pistachio solids.
5. In a separate bowl, whisk together the egg yolks and the remaining sugar until pale and slightly thickened.
6. Slowly pour about 1/2 cup of the warm pistachio-infused milk-cream mixture into the egg yolks, whisking constantly to temper the eggs.
7. Gradually pour the tempered egg mixture back into the saucepan with the remaining milk-cream mixture, whisking constantly.
8. Cook the mixture over medium-low heat, stirring constantly with a wooden spoon or spatula, until it thickens slightly and coats the back of the spoon (about 170-175°F or 77-80°C on an instant-read thermometer). Do not let it boil.
9. Remove from heat and stir in the rosewater and a pinch of salt. Add a few drops of green food coloring if desired, to achieve a pistachio-like hue.
10. Let the mixture cool to room temperature, then cover the bowl with plastic wrap, pressing it directly onto the surface of the custard to prevent a skin from forming. Refrigerate until completely chilled, preferably overnight.

11. Once chilled, strain the custard through a fine-mesh sieve once more to ensure a smooth texture.
12. Churn the pistachio rosewater custard in an ice cream maker according to the manufacturer's instructions until it reaches a soft-serve consistency.
13. Transfer the pistachio rosewater gelato to an airtight container and freeze for at least 2 hours or until firm before serving.
14. Serve the pistachio rosewater gelato in chilled bowls or cones. You can garnish with a sprinkle of chopped pistachios or a drizzle of rose syrup for presentation, if desired.

Enjoy your homemade pistachio rosewater gelato, with its nutty richness and floral undertones, perfect for a sophisticated and exotic dessert experience!

Cherry Amaretto Gelato

Ingredients:

- 2 cups whole milk
- 1 cup heavy cream
- 1 cup pitted cherries, fresh or frozen
- 3/4 cup granulated sugar
- 4 large egg yolks
- 1/4 cup Amaretto liqueur
- Pinch of salt

Instructions:

1. In a medium saucepan, combine the whole milk, heavy cream, pitted cherries, and half of the sugar. Heat over medium heat, stirring occasionally, until the mixture just begins to simmer. Do not let it boil.
2. Once simmering, reduce the heat to low and let the mixture simmer gently for about 10-15 minutes, allowing the cherries to soften and release their juices. Stir occasionally.
3. Remove from heat and let the cherry mixture cool slightly. Transfer the mixture to a blender or food processor and blend until smooth. Strain the mixture through a fine-mesh sieve into a clean bowl to remove any solids. Press gently with a spoon to extract as much liquid as possible. Discard the solids.
4. In a separate bowl, whisk together the egg yolks and the remaining sugar until pale and slightly thickened.
5. Slowly pour about 1/2 cup of the warm cherry-infused milk-cream mixture into the egg yolks, whisking constantly to temper the eggs.
6. Gradually pour the tempered egg mixture back into the saucepan with the remaining cherry-infused milk-cream mixture, whisking constantly.
7. Cook the mixture over medium-low heat, stirring constantly with a wooden spoon or spatula, until it thickens slightly and coats the back of the spoon (about 170-175°F or 77-80°C on an instant-read thermometer). Do not let it boil.
8. Remove from heat and stir in the Amaretto liqueur and a pinch of salt.
9. Let the mixture cool to room temperature, then cover the bowl with plastic wrap, pressing it directly onto the surface of the custard to prevent a skin from forming. Refrigerate until completely chilled, preferably overnight.
10. Once chilled, strain the custard through a fine-mesh sieve once more to ensure a smooth texture.

11. Churn the Cherry Amaretto custard in an ice cream maker according to the manufacturer's instructions until it reaches a soft-serve consistency.
12. Transfer the Cherry Amaretto gelato to an airtight container and freeze for at least 2 hours or until firm before serving.
13. Serve the Cherry Amaretto gelato in chilled bowls or cones. You can garnish with a few whole cherries or a sprinkle of chopped almonds for presentation, if desired.

Enjoy your homemade Cherry Amaretto gelato, with its fruity sweetness and almond undertones, perfect for a luxurious and flavorful dessert!

Orange Campari Gelato

Ingredients:

- 2 cups whole milk
- 1 cup heavy cream
- Zest of 2 oranges
- 3/4 cup granulated sugar
- 1/4 cup Campari liqueur
- 4 large egg yolks
- Pinch of salt
- Orange food coloring (optional, for enhanced color)

Instructions:

1. In a medium saucepan, combine the whole milk, heavy cream, and orange zest. Heat over medium heat, stirring occasionally, until the mixture just begins to simmer. Do not let it boil.
2. Once simmering, remove from heat and cover. Let the orange zest steep in the milk-cream mixture for about 15-20 minutes to infuse the flavor. Stir occasionally to ensure even infusion.
3. After steeping, strain the mixture through a fine-mesh sieve into a clean bowl to remove the orange zest. Press gently with a spoon to extract as much liquid as possible. Discard the orange zest.
4. In a separate bowl, whisk together the egg yolks and the granulated sugar until pale and slightly thickened.
5. Slowly pour about 1/2 cup of the warm orange-infused milk-cream mixture into the egg yolks, whisking constantly to temper the eggs.
6. Gradually pour the tempered egg mixture back into the saucepan with the remaining milk-cream mixture, whisking constantly.
7. Cook the mixture over medium-low heat, stirring constantly with a wooden spoon or spatula, until it thickens slightly and coats the back of the spoon (about 170-175°F or 77-80°C on an instant-read thermometer). Do not let it boil.
8. Remove from heat and stir in the Campari liqueur and a pinch of salt. Add a few drops of orange food coloring if desired, to achieve a vibrant orange color.
9. Let the mixture cool to room temperature, then cover the bowl with plastic wrap, pressing it directly onto the surface of the custard to prevent a skin from forming. Refrigerate until completely chilled, preferably overnight.
10. Once chilled, strain the custard through a fine-mesh sieve once more to ensure a smooth texture.

11. Churn the Orange Campari custard in an ice cream maker according to the manufacturer's instructions until it reaches a soft-serve consistency.
12. Transfer the Orange Campari gelato to an airtight container and freeze for at least 2 hours or until firm before serving.
13. Serve the Orange Campari gelato in chilled bowls or cones. You can garnish with a twist of orange zest or a slice of orange for presentation, if desired.

Enjoy your homemade Orange Campari gelato, with its refreshing citrus flavors and subtle bitter notes, perfect for a sophisticated and memorable dessert!

Honey Ricotta Gelato

Ingredients:

- 2 cups whole milk
- 1 cup heavy cream
- 1 cup whole milk ricotta cheese
- 1/2 cup honey (adjust to taste)
- 4 large egg yolks
- Pinch of salt

Instructions:

1. In a medium saucepan, combine the whole milk, heavy cream, ricotta cheese, and honey. Heat over medium heat, stirring occasionally, until the mixture just begins to simmer. Do not let it boil.
2. Once simmering, reduce the heat to low and let the mixture simmer gently for about 5-7 minutes, stirring occasionally, to incorporate the ricotta and honey completely into the milk-cream mixture.
3. Remove from heat and let the mixture cool slightly.
4. In a separate bowl, whisk together the egg yolks until smooth.
5. Gradually pour about 1/2 cup of the warm ricotta-honey mixture into the egg yolks, whisking constantly to temper the eggs.
6. Gradually pour the tempered egg mixture back into the saucepan with the remaining ricotta-honey mixture, whisking constantly.
7. Cook the mixture over medium-low heat, stirring constantly with a wooden spoon or spatula, until it thickens slightly and coats the back of the spoon (about 170-175°F or 77-80°C on an instant-read thermometer). Do not let it boil.
8. Remove from heat and stir in a pinch of salt.
9. Let the mixture cool to room temperature, then cover the bowl with plastic wrap, pressing it directly onto the surface of the custard to prevent a skin from forming. Refrigerate until completely chilled, preferably overnight.
10. Once chilled, strain the custard through a fine-mesh sieve to ensure a smooth texture.
11. Churn the honey ricotta custard in an ice cream maker according to the manufacturer's instructions until it reaches a soft-serve consistency.
12. Transfer the honey ricotta gelato to an airtight container and freeze for at least 2 hours or until firm before serving.
13. Serve the honey ricotta gelato in chilled bowls or cones. You can garnish with a drizzle of honey or a sprinkle of chopped pistachios for presentation, if desired.

Enjoy your homemade honey ricotta gelato, with its creamy texture and delicate sweetness, perfect for a delightful and indulgent dessert!

Espresso Granita

Ingredients:

- 2 cups brewed espresso or strong coffee
- 1/2 cup granulated sugar (adjust to taste)
- Optional: whipped cream, chocolate shavings, or cocoa powder for serving

Instructions:

1. Brew 2 cups of espresso or strong coffee. You can use an espresso machine or a stovetop espresso maker for this.
2. While the espresso is still hot, stir in the granulated sugar until completely dissolved. Taste and adjust the sweetness if needed.
3. Pour the sweetened espresso into a shallow, freezer-safe dish or baking pan. The larger the surface area, the quicker the granita will freeze.
4. Place the dish in the freezer and let it freeze for about 1 hour. After 1 hour, use a fork to scrape and stir the mixture to break up any ice crystals that have formed around the edges.
5. Repeat this process every 30 minutes to 1 hour, scraping and stirring with a fork until the entire mixture is frozen and has a slushy consistency.
6. Once fully frozen and scraped into granules, serve the espresso granita immediately in chilled glasses or bowls.
7. Optionally, garnish with a dollop of whipped cream, a sprinkle of chocolate shavings, or a dusting of cocoa powder before serving.

Espresso granita is best enjoyed fresh and is perfect for cooling down on hot days or as a refreshing dessert after a meal.

Amarena Gelato (Sour Cherry)

Ingredients:

- 2 cups whole milk
- 1 cup heavy cream
- 1 cup Amarena cherries in syrup (available in jars)
- 3/4 cup granulated sugar
- 4 large egg yolks
- Pinch of salt

Instructions:

1. Drain the Amarena cherries, reserving the syrup. Roughly chop the cherries into smaller pieces.
2. In a medium saucepan, combine the whole milk, heavy cream, and half of the sugar. Heat over medium heat, stirring occasionally, until the mixture just begins to simmer. Do not let it boil.
3. Once simmering, remove from heat and stir in the chopped Amarena cherries and a pinch of salt. Let the mixture steep for about 15-20 minutes to infuse the flavor of the cherries.
4. After steeping, strain the mixture through a fine-mesh sieve into a clean bowl to remove the cherry solids. Press gently with a spoon to extract as much liquid as possible. Discard the solids.
5. In a separate bowl, whisk together the egg yolks and the remaining sugar until pale and slightly thickened.
6. Slowly pour about 1/2 cup of the warm cherry-infused milk-cream mixture into the egg yolks, whisking constantly to temper the eggs.
7. Gradually pour the tempered egg mixture back into the saucepan with the remaining cherry-infused milk-cream mixture, whisking constantly.
8. Cook the mixture over medium-low heat, stirring constantly with a wooden spoon or spatula, until it thickens slightly and coats the back of the spoon (about 170-175°F or 77-80°C on an instant-read thermometer). Do not let it boil.
9. Remove from heat and let the mixture cool to room temperature. Once cooled, cover the bowl with plastic wrap, pressing it directly onto the surface of the custard to prevent a skin from forming. Refrigerate until completely chilled, preferably overnight.
10. Once chilled, stir in 1/4 cup of the reserved Amarena cherry syrup to enhance the flavor and color (adjust amount to taste).

11. Churn the Amarena cherry custard in an ice cream maker according to the manufacturer's instructions until it reaches a soft-serve consistency.
12. Transfer the Amarena gelato to an airtight container and freeze for at least 2 hours or until firm before serving.
13. Serve the Amarena gelato in chilled bowls or cones. You can garnish with a few whole Amarena cherries on top for presentation, if desired.

Enjoy your homemade Amarena gelato, with its tangy cherry flavor and creamy texture, perfect for a unique and delightful dessert experience!

Zabaione Gelato

Ingredients:

- 6 large egg yolks
- 1/2 cup granulated sugar
- 1/2 cup Marsala wine (or another sweet dessert wine like Vin Santo)
- 1 cup whole milk
- 1 cup heavy cream
- Pinch of salt

Instructions:

1. In a heatproof bowl, whisk together the egg yolks and sugar until well combined and slightly thickened.
2. Place the bowl over a pot of simmering water (double boiler method), making sure the bottom of the bowl does not touch the water.
3. Gradually whisk in the Marsala wine, whisking constantly, until the mixture becomes thick and creamy. This process will take about 8-10 minutes. The mixture should coat the back of a spoon.
4. Remove the bowl from heat and let the Zabaione mixture cool to room temperature.
5. In a separate saucepan, heat the whole milk and heavy cream over medium heat until it just begins to simmer. Do not let it boil.
6. Gradually pour the warm milk-cream mixture into the cooled Zabaione mixture, whisking constantly until well combined.
7. Add a pinch of salt to enhance the flavors.
8. Let the mixture cool to room temperature, then cover the bowl with plastic wrap, pressing it directly onto the surface of the custard to prevent a skin from forming. Refrigerate until completely chilled, preferably overnight.
9. Once chilled, churn the Zabaione custard in an ice cream maker according to the manufacturer's instructions until it reaches a soft-serve consistency.
10. Transfer the Zabaione gelato to an airtight container and freeze for at least 2 hours or until firm before serving.
11. Serve the Zabaione gelato in chilled bowls or cones. You can garnish with a sprinkle of cocoa powder or grated chocolate for presentation, if desired.

Enjoy your homemade Zabaione gelato, with its luxurious flavor of Marsala wine and creamy texture, perfect for a classic Italian dessert experience!

www.ingramcontent.com/pod-product-compliance
Lightning Source LLC
LaVergne TN
LVHW081615060526
838201LV00054B/2268